IN SOLITUDE & SOLACE

Compiled By

StoryMirror

First Edition: June 2019
Printed in India

ISBN: 978-93-88698-06-1

Printed at Dhote Offset Printer, Mumbai
Typeset in Garamond

Cover Desiagn: Prashant Gopal Gurav

STORYMIRROR
Stories that reflect you

Publisher: StoryMirror Infotech Pvt. Ltd.
145, First Floor, Powai Plaza, Hiranandani Gardens, Powai, Mumbai - 400076, India

Web: https://storymirror.com
Facebook: https://facebook.com/storymirror
Twitter: https://twitter.com/story_mirror
Instagram: https://instagram.com/storymirror

About the Author

Akshatha Ilangovan is an Aerospace Engineer who writes poetry to escape reality and to make sense of it. In 2015, her poem "She's Human!" was published in The Anonymous Writer website. She was a content writer at the Blooming Beacon for The StreetStore '15 Event held in Chennai. In 2017, she started her Instagram page 'The Rime of Lines' (@rime_of_lines) where she posts her artwork along with her writing. Apart from writing, she enjoys singing, pencil sketching and travelling. Currently, Akshatha is pursuing her Masters in International Business in Zurich, Switzerland.!

The Reverie of Irreverence

By Akshatha Ilangovan

The starry light lighting up
A truss in the crane,
Is all I can see through the grill
Outside the window,
Gazing hard at which
I think no thought
And at that fraction,
I think of you.
Those earnest bespectacled eyes.

In the silence
Of the songs that play
Right in my ears,
I stare at the table
Straight far down,
And glance back at my books
Only to see words,
Words I know
That suddenly seem strange
The way they have been
Spelt?

I remember telling you both
How I can study with music
In my ears.

But I can't.
In fact, not until I forget
There is something playing.
Haven't told you this, either.
How I experience an escape
In the beats that play on
Recklessly,
Unafraid, lurking in the centre of my ear.
A loss of the burden
Wrapping around everything
That I have to study now.
A solace,
That carries away the disgust
That creeps in,
No matter how much I forbid it.

There are moments
I have had with each song.
Moments that rally a wave of
Emotions I could never have
Anyone ever understand.
You warn me of long-term deafness,
But the promise of an eternal
Music in my mind
Deters me from
Listening.

But some days I put away
Those headphones
And stay
With an unsettling feeling -
Incomplete, unexpressed, and undone.

Love that knew no fear
Struggles today in an unfamiliar hand
That strikes
The chord of authority.
A baritone I once adored,
Today sinks in phone calls
I rush through with a 'take care'
That I wonder if I mean.
And the first voice I hear
Is silenced in rebukes I wish
I could bite my tongue
From uttering.

Love is not scanty
From you
Or me...
But only a lack of patience,
To try and see.
An apology may heal,
But time will undoubtedly reveal
A respite that we shall reach.
An answer that we seek...
As a family

About the Author

Bijal, a creative content writer in the field of education for little more than half a decade, writes stories and poetries that touch people's lives and make an impact. As part of her professional requirements, she writes storyboards that make difficult socio-political concepts easy and engaging for the readers. Her educational background in social science makes her a complete people's person. A writer in 4 languages, her writings can be read on www.signingonandoff.blogspot.in. Most of her writings have an overwhelming feel of strong women and compassion.

Searching For You!

By Bijal Pandya

The day we last met
Did I say I love you?
The day we last met
Did I know I love you?

The day we last met
Did I say I'll miss you?
The day we last met
Did I know I will long to see you?

I don't know if I did know any of these,
I don't know and now I freeze,
I don't know when shall we meet again,
I don't know, but life passes by in this bargain.

I live with you in my dream,
I share with you my coffee's cream,
I talk to you as if you are across the table,
I want you now before I walk the aisle.

The smell of those coffees still strong and nice,
The meetings we had talking all from cheese to mice,
You laughing at me as I got tired of the show,
You admiring me as I wear my frankness as a bow,

The warmth of your hands, wrapped around my palm,
The affection in your eyes, that made me so calm,
You made my life so warm and loved,
As memories ignite, I miss being gloved.

You showed to me many a lights,
You taught me to jump to glory despite plights,
For you I took that courage on,
For you it is, that on my head a feather I don.

I took many a flights in search of you,
I took many a wisdom to search for you,
I hear of you gathering glory around,
But, I long to hear the caring sound.

I am happy you are what you wanted to be,
I am happy I see you as I wanted to see,
But o dear take me on your flight and wear me on your sleeve,
I promise for then in pain you will never have to heave.

As I move ahead and get lost in the crowd,
I try each inch to make you feel proud,
Now on the aisle that I will soon be,
I wish I have you around for me...

About the Author

Arvind has been writing novellas, short stories and poetry since his college days and has had his articles published in many e-zines. A telecommunications IT professional with a computer engineering background, he has been actively involved in many creative initiatives at work and has been on the editorial panel of many corporate e-zines. With a keen interest in human emotions, the wonder of science and an element of magic realism, his works try to find a balance between the real and the fantastical. He is also an active sketch artist, drawing inspiration from Renaissance masters like El Greco and Da Vinci. You may learn more about his writing and sketches at https://arvindiyer27.wordpress.com

A Beautiful Mind

By Arvind Iyer

The deep dark alleys of the mind, long and unwinding
to thc core,
A few we know so well, some, yet to explore,

Beautiful memories of yesterday are hidden in a shrine,
Yet there are those that hurt, it's a bittersweet galore.

There's a search for some answers yet a few questions arise,
The need to forget some, but the urge to know more,
And a few virgin by-lanes, a mystery to the core.

A few dark desires, some shine with a light divine,
An unending noise in some, a few ring with a melodic chime,

There's a will to succeed yet the weakness to give in to crime,
There's a belief in eternity yet the fear of running out of time.

Secrets dwell deep inside, never shall they come to the fore,
A needless hate for some, yet there are those we adore,

A sense of wonder, a moment of fear,
A subconscious smile, a forced tear,

They're all treasured, emotions of every kind,
It's a treacherous place, yet a beautiful mind.

About the Author

Jai is as passionate about creative writing as he is about information technology, the industry he has been in for almost two decades now. With an Advanced English certification from Cambridge University, he has also worked as a freelance Language Editor. A post-graduate in Computer Applications, Jai is intensely passionate about writing and the English language itself, only next to his love for computers and programming. While writing, he often likes to create alchemy of logic and imagination to create his own narration style. He maintains a blog at http://kreativpitcher.blogspot.com where he presents his stories, poems, pencil sketches and photography.

The Floating Mist

By Jai Ganesh Vaidyanathan

Who is this floating mist?
Who comes and steals my dream,
Numbing my senses, scaring my wits,
Paralyzing me, and I cannot scream.

Who is this dame; what is her name?
Am I the one she is calling?
Will she let go, or will she hold me?
Will she save my life from falling?

She puts me to sleep, by waking me up,
I am gasping for air; I cannot breathe,
She captivates me; makes me sweat,
My sanity is pretty much freaked.

She scares me; she encompasses me,
I jump from my solitude into my life,
I am split in two, by fighting within,
My days are spent in strife.

In my crowded days, when I open my eyes
I see her as my scenic dream,
In my lonely nights, when I close my eyes
I dream her up in my dark reality.

My life's become black and white,
With so many colours splashed in,
I bathe in her light; feel her warmth,
I am now cleansed from within.

I reach out to her, hold her hands,
I want to tell that I am fine,
But she must not come, into my dreams,
For my dark nights are only mine.

She only smiles, looks into my eyes,
I see my lonely life in there,
She whispers to me, says we are one,
And she is always there to care.

Days I spent, searching for true love,
Now I know it is she,
I will protect her; even kill for her,
Even if the person to die is me.

About the Author

Nibedita is a senior business journalist by profession but writer at heart. Her work can be found on FranchiseIndia.com and her personal blogs can be found on Tumblr.com. She pursued Journalism from Indian Institute of Journalism and New Media, Bangalore, to get a better understanding of human emotions and stories that go uncovered on daily basis. She loves travelling, watching all kinds of movies and reading literature. She is still exploring different styles, genres and technicalities in articulating thoughts, spinning ideas and penning them down

Get Me A Home

By Nibedita Mohanta

Get me a home,
Where I can keep,
All my childhood memories.
All my tiny little broken dreams,
So that I can mend them now.

Get me a home,
So that I can treasure my moments.
Moments, when my mother used to smile on my achievements.
Moments, when my father was proud of me.
Moments, when I was the most valuable treasure of my brother.

Get me a home,
Where I can see me doing all that I couldn't.
Smiles, which have faded from my lips.
Tears, that have dried on my cheeks.
Laughter, which oncs used to be my strength.

Get me a home,
Where I can hold back the time.
Time, when new pen was the world's best gift from my dad.
Time, when mom's handmade cake was the delicious present
on my birthday.
Time, when my brother fought with his best friend for me.

Get me a home,
Where I can relive the moments I miss.
Where I can cry my heart out.
Where I am always the special person at least for me.

Can you??

About the Author

Preeti is a software professional. Writing lets her be more expressive than she is in reality and helps her stay at peace in this chaotic world. Not only poetry, she also likes to write journals and articles on varied subjects, driven from personal experiences. She also enjoys writing micro tales and wishes to explore more of prose and fiction/story writing. She is an ardent reader and an active blogger too.

And You Too... Left!

By Preeti Lolla

You seemed to be that ray of little hope,
When I struggled looking for the lost sheen,
Transforming into someone I rarely had been,
Smiling, chuckling, positive and all glee,

Happiness felt beautiful, yet so strange,
A simple question always made my day,
For all fears just appeared to be at bay,
Surprised to find such rare connection,
Making peace with the inherent commotion,

Awestruck at how well you could read my mind,
Conversations had been just so much manifold,
The bonding that I felt only grew stronger,
Only to find again my little world shatter,

The pieces of my soul I somehow gathered,
Had once again been not-so-unexpectedly withered,
Those unexpressed feelings did stay,
Even when you silently chose to walk away,

Unguided but stronger as I chose to evolve,
Had no other way but to resolve,
To never let my life be shrouded,
By the darkness you left!

About the Author

Ria is a faculty of Business English and Intercultural communication at TCS. She taught Engineering/Management students Business Communication before joining TCS in 2011. Ria has an MPhil (Women's Studies), a BEd and is pursuing her PhD (Jadavpur University). She won the Italian Govt. Scholarship; Commonwealth Fellowship (UK); IATEFL-BESIG and Melbourne University Conference scholarships to study/present. She has papers on Business English, Life-Skills, Employability skills, Women and Law, Gender in the classroom and Experiential Learning. Ria speaks English, Bengali, Hindi and Italian. She is a trained dancer, pianist and vocalist and loves travelling and performing arts.

Elixir

By Ria Mukherjee

Petrichor!
The word rang
Inside her mind
Like a bell.
The echoes
Reverberated
In an atmosphere
Of nostalgia
And stillness
Like a
Few frozen drops
Of wisdom
And sadness.

The smell
Of the damp
Wet earth
After the rains
Brought up memories
Of lost loves
That had once
Seemed like the
Manifestations
Of divine happiness.
Narratives of bliss

Reminiscences
So eternal, infinite
And timeless!

Drowning
In the headiness
Of love,
Drinking
It endlessly
Like ambrosia.
Soaking
In the attention
Of the lover in frenzy,
Sinking
In the arms
Of the beloved
In ecstasy.
Living through days
Of enchanted bliss.
In a state of magic
That had seemed
Like a dizzy
Spell of euphoria.
Every moment
Created a history
Of a poignant memory.

Yet,
It all ended.
In a big
Wide chasm
Of heaviness
And a dull

And quiet
Darkness.
Like a void
Of space
In breathlessness
In a rhythm
Of peace
And restlessness.
It left behind
Bitter sweet memories
And a deep
Loneliness.

Memories
Of a distant
Utopia
Which was
Once so dear
Even now
Seemed near.
It struck a chord
Somewhere
In the
Innermost core
Of her heart.
The note was pure
And it
Left her longing
For more.

Saudade!
The wisdom
From an awareness
Of the presence
Of an absence

Filled the essence
Of her mind.
Like a sip
Of elixir
That had
Seemingly
Lifted the tragic
Curtain of a crisis.
A vision of
The cycle of life
Rose like a spectre
Suddenly
Before her eyes
Like an illumination.
An anagnorisis.

An enchanting symphony
Of light and darkness
Enveloped her
Subliminal non existence.
A transcendental melody
Filled and fulfilled
Equally her being
And her non being.
It brought into harmony
The mortality
Of her existence
As well as the Elixir
Of her
Divine Immortality.

About the Author

Akash is a corporate banker with a private bank for last 4 years. He successfully balances writing complicated and technical business proposals along with creative writing and poetry. Being an empanelled writer at Sportskeeda, he has published 20 articles garnering over 1 lakh reads. Though he belongs from a small town in Bihar, his heart belongs to Delhi having spent 5 years in DU. He is a diehard foodie and TV shows fanatic with a huge 3 TB hard disk collection. His inspiration arises from his unrelenting pursuit of love despite numerous heartbreaks.

Just Wanna Be With You

By Akash Anand

I have been waiting for this moment, I have waited far too long
I don't know if I could ever write you a song
But now you are by my side and I am the happiest person alive
Never thought my dreams would come true
I just wanna be with you.

Be it summer, be it fall, I would hold you in my arms
You are the brightest star in the sky, baby I won't ever
let you cry.
I will make all your wishes come true, I just wanna be with you.
You are there in my heart, we won't ever be apart.
I want to see you say 'I do' and I would never let you go,
All the things I said are true, I just wanna be with you.

But now it's time to come back to life, I know it's all a lie
You are not there by my side, My dreams won't ever come true
I will never be with you.

About the Author

Chan CarTee AKA Chandru is a budding writer, who has been writing articles, short stories and poems for over 2 years, He provides creative, abstract writing and content editing. By profession, a Software Engineer, his short writings are first motivated by his family and friends (MAcMYKLS) and he started working on many topics and participated in many writing contests. His writing skills is confirmed independently on https://storymirror.com. He especially known as Gallivanter, Foodie and additionally, he enjoys doing pencil sketches. You may learn more about his writing services at Goodmenproject.com

The Wave Girl

By Chan CarTee

I am glad that I met you, like a sagar and shore,
That Sagar is blue with little white waves,
Blue, as for as your eyes,
White waves like your smile,
These waves are so special, it hugs the shore indefinitely,
Same way, I wish you always hugged by arms of goodness.

Sometimes, you may hate me,
But don't forget to remember me,
Maybe this hate you give is my hope to live,
I too hate you, to the hate you give, but
Inversely, I wanna replace the hate with love always.

I wish you that, may you always have a shell in your pocket,
And sand on your path, as my remembrance,
Come spent sometime before you go,
Only with, You, me and your words,
Wish my wishes comes true by your name,
Wish me a wish... My Wave Girl.

About the Author

Ishan Choudhary is an MBBS graduate from Zaporozhye State Medical University, Ukraine, and currently pursuing post graduate degree in ENT & Head and Neck Surgery from Medanta The Medicity Hospital, Gurugram. For him poetry is the only escape from the mediocrity of routine life, he wrote a lot of poems for his college and school magazine. His days, years, life has seen pleasure and pain, sunshine and darkness, so one half of his writing is about ecstasy of the nature, beauty of life, the magic of human imagination it's about unicorns, butterflies, rainbows the other part of his writing is about numbness of human existence, aching of our soul, loneliness of human heart that we all hide behind our smiles. He feels if his poetry is able to ignite a little spark in someone's darkness if he can give a little hope to a dying soul, then he has made it as an artist.

If I Never See You Again

By Ishan Choudhary

If I never see you again
I will keep you safe in the corner of my eyes
Paint you on the walls of my heart
Stare at you for hours and hours

I will smell your essence in scent of pouring rain
Feel your touch in tenderness of a new born baby
See your shine in the bright moonlight
I will get drunk every night and write you in my poems
I will keep you with me forever till eternity.

About the Author

Rahul has been hiking the Himalayas solo since past 4 years. It was while climbing the mountains he got inspired to write about the colours of life experiences and people he met down the road. He mostly writes poems and stories when he works in City where he believes the rebellion in people to live free or to fight against the slavery of 9 - 5 job has been replaced by the fancy bonanzas. Currently, he helps people to bring their offline store or idea, online by creating websites. Find out more about him at www.trekeazy.com.

The Violet Killer

By Rahul Khati

I found a garden of flowers in the wild,
But it was the violet that I chose.
It remembered me of you,
So I picked one and never let it loose.

It was the brightest,
Just like you,
Still I plucked it and made it sad,
Like I did to you.

All I wanted was a violet for you,
Did I do wrong?
Certainly it was you that I was searching in everything,
So shall I leave the blame on you?

I never wanted you to tell,
It's the violet that wanted you to know.
You were more violet that day,
Beautiful than the one,
I may never know, I know.

Yet it was your vibe
Which made the violet hide.
Oh love! I survived your eyes,
But the violet died.

About the Author

Shibani has been working as a Software professional at Tata Consultancy Services for seven years. She has always been an avid reader and that gave her inspiration for writing. She was always a bright student with good writing abilities which was confined to her school magazines only. She has always been appreciated by her family and friends for her writings so she was encouraged to publish her writing for the very first time to such a larger audience. This is the first time she has published her writing and is really excited for people's response.

Alas! It Was A Mere DREAM

By Shibani Nanda

In the realm of my dream..
You were the ruling prince..
Riding the chariot of love..
You took me away in a blink..

Such a treat was our Castle of glass..
That had only two of us on its walls..
Reflecting the Rays of our emotions..
Devoid of all worldly commotions..

You, the prince, took up your duties to the throne..
With jewel studded crown, you were sworn..
Struck by the aura around you, my king..
Me, your princess, already felt like the queen..

Together we conquered all hearts..
Building our kingdom of all smiles..
Never dropped a tear of sorrow..
Joy was sprinkled all over, till miles and miles..

But one day, It was such horrifying..
With a sense of tiredness, I was lying..
Neither the Castle, nor you were there, my king..
Alas!! It was a mere dream...

About the Author

Vashita Madan, a Masters student from Delhi is currently in her final year of study. She also has a bachelor's degree in journalism. She performs spoken word poetry as often as she attends food festivals around her city. She has previously been published in a Penguin anthology. She may be reached at @vashitaaa on Instagram, where she primarily shares her work.

An Ode To Me

By Vashita Madan

I'm done

Telling you how I feel,
Letting you in
On my secrets
And my past.

You promised
To stay,
To make it right,
To make it last.

Heard me scream,
Saw me cry,
A man so patient,
Gentle and kind,
I thought you were the one,
For you let me speak my mind.

I emptied my heart
Right out to you,
I believed you
When you said it'll be fine,
A man so gentle,
Patient and kind,
I thought you were the one,
For you let me speak my mind.

And then I saw you
Opening the door,
Tiptoeing out,
Hoping I won't hear,
Praying I don't see.

And that day
I realised,
You wouldn't have made it right,
No one ever will,
Till I don't love myself,
I'll ache and be broken still.

About the Author

Amit Kumar works with a leading Public Sector Bank in Chennai. He writes mainly on topics related to self-development and personal growth. After studying and working in various parts of the country, Amit utilizes his experiences to approach topics from various angles and expresses himself through articles or poetry. He has been winner of first prize in a poetry competition in his current organization. Amit has contributed to https://storymirror.com and posts his thoughts on his blog http://persistenceisthesecret.blogspot.in/.

Life's Open Secret

By Amit Kumar

It doesn't move the way you want,
It doesn't choose the way you want,
It goes the way it's written there,
It moves the way it's driven there,

You let it know it'll change the track,
You move with it, it'll fill your rack,
Sometimes dreams sometimes nightmares,
It'll bring forth you whoever cares,

It can be fun it can be terrible,
It's a big canvas if you make it simple,
To face the simple, you need to take blow,
However dense, you need to look through,

Tough can be tough but can't be rough,
Until you don't play, your heart a bluff,
You need to love; you need to hate,
Only a sip won't tell the real taste,

Dare to dream, dare to follow,
Be ready to fall but never be a shadow,
Sometimes down some times up,
Wherever you are don't ever give up,
Once you make that clear it would come with you,
You then be the driver, let it travel with you!

About the Author

Chaitali Bose Bhattacharjee is a Content Editor & Strategist, Web Columnist and top Blogger who worked with leading media agencies. She did a major in English and management in Marketing & Communication Strategy. Her works are published in varied deemed publications like TOI, Indian Express, Huffingtonpost India, Soulspot, Oddity, Indiblogger, Narrow Road journal and is part of two international multilingual anthology of poems. The Stimulants for her writings are race, equality, gender, empathy, connections, life in itself; which flock together hoping to find a voice not always conclusive, but sometimes inquisitive too. She occasionally conducts creative writing workshops and does poetry reading for the community kids, which gives comfort to her fidgety heart.

My Conscience

By Chaitali Bhattacharjee

Closed mind
Prejudiced heart
Eyes of apathy
Rules of creed
Sounds of reluctance
Nothing can fence me.

Mortal passions
Morbid arguments
Endorsed ideas
Self pretensions
Accepted rituals
Nothing can harness me.

I am free.
As free as birds of wings,
As free as the air that swings,
As free as music that afloat,
As free as the waves on the blue
and the rising embers across the shore.

The conflict between –
The agreeable and disagreeable
unties the conscious within.
The phoenix rises from the frame,
I am your *conscience* to reclaim.

About the Author

Chinmoy Bhattacharjee is an IT Consultant, working with Tata Consultancy Services for nearly 18 years. He holds an Engineering degree from National Institute of Technology, Kurukshetra. In between the pressures of performing leadership roles in his busy corporate life, Chinmoy writes short stories, essays and poetry. Chinmoy reads extensively, loves travelling and plays the guitar. He currently lives with his family in Gurgaon.

The Peddler's Meal

By Chinmoy Bhattacharjee

Barefoot he hobbled, on the scorched tarmac floor.
Wincing in pain, shuffling from door to door.
Though bent over in pain, proud was his gait.
Not alms he sought, he peddled petty freight.
He knocked and waited, expectations in his eyes.
Pity he did not seek. For his goods, a just price!
Him I saw not. Nor the dignity of his chore.
Unfeeling, unseeing eyes - conditioned to ignore.

Too many on these streets, a society ill at ease;
Dehumanized and exploited, a cursed incurable disease.
He had mere moments, until the lights turned green.
Seeking hope, seeking succour. His vision sharp and keen.
"Buy his goods". Fervently, she nudged.
Startled, I beckoned. And hither the old man trudged.
"Ear buds, Sir", he implored. "None better than these.
And quite reasonable too, a mere twenty rupees!"

I dared not bargain, her stern visage I espied.
And paid him his dues, for the needless goods he plied.
My frowns persisted; would this purchase I repent?
Wasted money, or worse, not worth a red cent?
He paused for a moment, his relief fighting to conceal.
And said, "This first sale will provide for my meal"!
She judged him not. Only she saw his pride.
One illumined heart, where compassion doth reside.

About the Author

Nandita has been working as a creative writer, blogger and a poet for over six years though she wrote her first short story and first poem at the age of 9 years and has had a steady relationship with the writing world since then. Her 20 odd years as a consumer behaviour specialist and brand planner has also given her insights into the corporate world, while her personal interests in healing, spiritual coaching and teaching management students has given her a broad base from which to approach many topics and mindsets. She provides content writing, life skills, spiritual writing and creative writing services. Her writing services and skills may be seen in platforms like https://nanditawritesblog.wordpress.com, her coffee blog - kaappiconversations.blogspot.com, Spiritualcruiser.com, HeadHonchos.com. She has also been exposed to script writing from MFA, Dubai and her varied professional, personal experiences and international stints have provided rich sources for creative pieces. She especially enjoys writing content pieces based on life experiences and stories inspired by reality.

I am

By Nandita Kaushik

Who I really am
Hides deep inside of me
Protected, shielded from lies
From what the world wants to believe

I will emerge when it is time
When my soul says all is fine
But will it be too late
Will the face outside be the one within

Will I wait for guarantees
Will I take the step today
This is all I think about night and day
The answer lies deep within it says

Reveal yourself with no return
Maybe there is light maybe none
Just the freedom is enough
No duality, no conflict to be done

I write, I create, I heal
Truth this is if you believe
Waiting a chance to be seen
To be known, to be complete

Me in my world of creation
Where I belong heart and soul
My only inspiration, my salvation.

About the Author

Aditya Thakur has been writing for two of his instagram pages since his freshmen year at Pec University of Technology, Chandigarh. His poems and articles center around the themes of solitude, youth, teen-melodrama & elements of escapism and explorations. Currently pursuing Bachelors in Electrical Engineering, Aditya is most fulfilled when growing professionally and personally, likewise. In addition to writing, he is an avid follower of Alternative Rock, hip hop, EDM & Electropop and likes to paint and draw in his free time. Follow him on Instagram at @_adi_thakur, @the_footloose_teenager & @the_red_euphoria.

The Rush Of Your Dreams

By Aditya Thakur

A few unsettling attempts and
a criss-cross of otherworldly debts,
An urge to rush up a storm and
downright pushing down the trends.
Raging against the sea storms &
falling off the tallest peaks in a silent sleep,
Life's a fortress of your deeds in the reign of your dreams.

When every road you ever took,
tosses you right into the crashes
Rise like a sacred phoenix,
after you burn down to your ashes.
Look a little deep within and
you'll always find a buried visage,
That whirls and Spirits you through a world
built out of monotony's wreckage.

Running through the strangest lanes and
walking across the most unfamiliar bridges,
You'd find one moment in time when
all horizons are held through loose stitches.
Drink to the magic and the enigma, and
the fantasies of it all ending,
Or to a witch hunt in the seven heavens,
when you make past the flashy lightning.

Dreaming within dreams and
knitting a few false inceptions,
Play risks with your fate and
Fuck people who live in fractions.
Wrongs and rights will always fall in lanes and
your tears will be all there to witness.
Cause it's the lone wolves who work fires and
breathe life into existence.

Though you'll bleed of guilt and
wail cause of all the tragedies and the regrets,
Don't ever sit scared or live a life
soaking in the drops of death.
Turn your power into rage and
pass your rage to your faith and actions,
So liberate yourself with silver wings, and
win your own gold redemption.

About the Author

Adya Ghoshal is an amateur writer who is a student of 12th std. Along with her studies she has been contributing equally to her writing skills. She has been with StoryMirror for years now and had already contributed her poems to "poignant painters" the initiative taken by StoryMirror towards published books. Also she had completed her "52 weeks challenge" organised by StoryMirror by submitting her 52 original poems along the year 2018. Along with being active on StoryMirror, she represents her work quite regularly on "your quotes". She also has a Facebook page named "A pen, a paper and a dream" where you can visit to know more about her and her work. She has also been interested in writing plays and had acted in one of her own plays named "An empty chair" in a theatre workshop held in Lucknow. She usually uses simple English in her poems to make it easier for her readers spread across the geography. "Simple and effective" is the motto Adya follows to take her readers for a ride into her world!

The Wake-Up Song

By Adya Ghoshal

Night time and a hush all over,
The moon was shinning bright,
The stars were there, all prepared,
To dance throughout the night.

Everyone was sleeping,
Inside their four walls,
When the music hit the ears,
The earth shook, the walls melted,
And everyone ran in fear.

We all gathered together,
And witnessed the strange plight,
It was not in the scheduled list,
Was it the mistake of our guide?

The earth kept shaking,
The buildings crashed down,
The world was ending,
For all the walls were now gone!
The plants grew out,
And soared high in sky,
Birds sang along,
And began to fly.

The earth stopped shaking,
And the fear was now gone,
The animals too joined in,
And everyone danced along.

The rain started,
And we broke the remaining walls,
No one was now divided,
And everyone gathered around,
Religion, caste, war, race,
All melted with the rain,
The beautiful song,
Kept its pace,
And there was no pain.

The Moon shone brightly,
And astonished were all,
When they saw the universe dancing in the sky,
The stars raced and jumped,
Twirling with the song,
They melted their sparkles and coloured us all,
The sea waves turned and made us cry along,
The water washed away the hatred,
And love flowed through us in its purest form!

Hand in hand, all laughed together,
Under the sky of a billion stars,
We all hugged and enjoyed the strange weather,
For that night love made us ONE!

Now we knew how stupid we were,
To build up walls, and fill them with hate,
As we cried at each other's shoulder,
We realized what true love is,

WE ALL ARE SAME!
WE ALL ARE ONE!
The one who divided us were now crushed!

We laughed at ourselves,
And danced again,
But then the light came;
The alarm rang, we woke up,
Inside our four walls,
Scorching heat outside,
Polluted, corrupted world,
I looked at my watch,
It was time to run again,
But what was that dream all about?

Hatred took birth again,
The speechless were crushed,
The walls divided us again,
For we were too blind to see the truth,
And too scared to taste true love!

So until we Wake Up,
Slave we were,
Are,
And will always remain!

About the Author

Anubhuti is a BA in Political Science & has a degree in MSW as well as LLB. She has 10 years of experience in working with NGOs that are active in different walks of life. She has also worked in various courts. Through reading & research, travels & work experience, she has gained a multitude of exposures, which she tries to imbibe in her writings. She has aptitude for writing short poems & stories in English & Hindi / Urdu on diverse issues of her interests. Moreover she has a disposition to research on subjects that fascinate and captivate her. These writings have been published on her social media handles as well as on her blogging site & have been appreciated by literary groups which encourages her to venture into full time writing.

It Is Raw..Shall We Draw..

By Anubhuti Singhal

The canvas is blank,
We can't leave it vacant.
It is raw..Shall we draw?

The canvas there..is not meant to remain bare,
Had it so been intended,
The methods to have it filled,
Would not have originated.

Empty it will look bleak, designed it will look sleek,
Let us choose the style,
Pastel or enamel..ink or oil?
Former or latter?
It really doesn't matter,
But the painting should look better.

The pencil is here,
Let us sketch it black or grey.
The color is here,
Let us paint from the brush or spray,
The purpose is to create some work fine,
To gladden the heart of mine.
Even if it is not picture perfect..Even if it has some defect,
This will be the find,
That will please the mind.
Acknowledgement is not the goal,
It is the contentment of the soul.

About the Author

Ashish Chawla is a freelance writer, storyteller, poet, and songwriter, pursuing a Bachelor's Degree in Pharmacy, currently in his final year. He is also pursuing a Diploma in Film and Television Direction, to mould a career in directing films. His keen interest in writing and a passion for storytelling has given him a chance to experiment with his writing skills, write on a variety of genres, thereby expanding his vocabulary and vocational skills, an eventually a keen and patient audience. His previous work can be found on thisisashish18.wordpress.com.

Hide & Seek

By Ashish Chawla

A smile is what you see, the sadness is what I hide.
I wish I could flee, into the sky that is so wide.

My heart won't close its doors to stop the pain;
And my screams won't cross the walls of my brain.
Though I've tried so hard to confide in myself;
Being lonely, sometimes, makes me want to jump off a train.

Perfection is what you see, mistakes are what I hide.
I wish I could flee, into the sky that is so wide.

I am done with this life of sorrow, and trying to pretend;
However beautiful it may be, it has now started to descend.
But if there was any opportunity for me to grab;
I would have given everything for my life to ascend.

Laughter is what you see, tears are what I hide.
I wish I could flee, into the sky that is so wide.

The future I'll be living, may somehow be bright;
At the end of the tunnel, there will always be light.
Even though the time for me has stopped;
I will keep on searching for the one to kiss and say good night.

Results are what you'll see, dreams are what I'll hide.
I won't flee into the sky, even if it is so wide.

About the Author

Seeing the beauty in little and simple things fascinated her to write about the things which meant something. **Himanshi** started creating stories since she got perceptive about imagination which is, there is nothing perceptive about Imagination and the theory that somehow, somewhere it is happening in this world or another held her moment to get in writing while studying in school. The one accomplice and the source of courage to keep her writing, are books which realized her in the beginning that "Struggle is the sarcasm which introduces us to the reality of life with the solace". The specialty about her work is that despite being such short experienced, her work is more lifelike and encompasses the ability to let the reader see beyond the lines. For her, happiness is the shimmer for writing and her belief in writing is that "if the work is worthy of you, it will begin with a smile and if it ends with a smile, it will last to take you higher".

Dreams To Die For

By Himanshi

Strange road,
You will declare "the road you thought you knew your whole life, turned out to be strange"
But it's the path which will lead me to my dream world

And
I will say "if I have the COURAGE, I will start my journey"
Will come across a forest of so many trees large, small, wide,
You will say with celerity "that's nice,
you can start your world here"
But I know that my place is a will-o'-the-wisp
I will say to myself "KEEP GOING"
Will see desolate, a morbid forest,
You will say in ado "there is no hope for you further than this"

And
I will say "if I have the will, I will make myself STRONG ENOUGH for the struggle"
Will come across a dead end,
You will say in aggravation "how far will you go?
maybe you should go back"

And
I will say "if I dare, I will make my own path
because I know, across it,
where the LAND MEETS THE SKY
is where my reverie lies"

I will swim across deep water,
walk on the avenged road,
climb up the mountains and silent valleys
Will see the FAERIE with thousands of trees and
millions of dreams,
You will say while vexing
"there is not any sign of your world here"
But I want to live in my world my own dreams, my creation,
not in the one which others created for their dream and
I will fall not in desperation but.. in my thoughts

And
I will stand to say this loud
"if I have the courage and I know I have because
I have come this far and I will dream,
I will SAW THE SEED of my tree of the dream"
Will see the roots CLENCHING the earth,
You will say in woe "there is no place for you,
they are the VENERABLE tree of dreams"
I will look around to see other's world but
I will find the motivation for DRUDGERY and
be HALE and RUGGED

And
I will shout "if I have the strength,
then I will nurture, nurture my tree to makes the roots to go
DEEPEST OF DEEP"
You will grow aggro and say "you have lost your mind,
others have the ENORMOUS and PRODIGIOUS
tree of dreams"
But this is all that my mind thinks of,
every night I lie in bed the brightest color fill my head

I will say "if I have the patience, I will LET IT GROW,
I will let it go as much as high and widest of wide"

You will make me look around and ask
"they are too much high,
how can you survive between them?"
I will see at the sky,
And shout, shout loud "if I have the courage,
I will DREAM BIG, big enough that even
they wouldn't be able to see the alp of my tree of the dream"

But
I know my tree, my dream and I will know where
the ZENITH of my dream tree lies in that HIGH SKY,
full of dreams
Will pass the dusk.. enter in the night,
You will say in tremble "you cannot see in the dark,
you do not know what's coming"
I will smile and look at the GLEAMING stars
and EFFULGENT sky,
And say "I am not a STRANGER TO THE DARK
and I know that that DAWN is coming"
You will shout out loud in temper "all I want you to have a
SAFE and TENDED future and this place is not safe,
what you want is impossible, they will kill you
with your tree of the dream"

And I will answer so all will hear the tallest to the oldest
"this is my work, my creation, this is my inception,
THIS IS MY DREAM and I have come this far to forge, to
design and stand in my world, I will do everything
that is possible before the impossible arrives to turn this
DREAM INTO REALITY and I will not let anyone take this
away from me because I have the courage,
TO BE IMPERVIOUS, the courage to
LIVE FOR MY DREAM and
DIE FOR MY DREAM".

About the Author

Shruthi Venkat is a product design student in Bangalore. She has been writing poetry since her school days. She has always been inclined to art, be it poetry, painting or photography. She also performs spoken word in her free time. She has published various articles and also been a part of an anthology of poems launched at the Bangalore Literary Festival. She enjoys writing narrative poetry, where the poem flows with a storyline and creates a visual portrayal.

Sunshine

By Shruthi Venkat

As I wake up and peep out of my cage,
I see the war has come to an end.
They've finally run out of rage,
And found ways to mend.
Debris from buildings and broken toys
Lay around, just as a remainder.

My head sorta misses the violent noises
Only now can people actually begin to ponder.
The destruction is immense,
The mental aftermath even worse.
The new spring air still feels tense,
It's like we've been freed from an endless curse.

As the first Ray of light,
Hits the doomed town,
Something still doesn't seem just right,
Clearly everyone's got a frown.
Acres of dry land shimmers in shades of Brown.
The pastel and dull shades adorn the walls.

Colors seem to have lost a meaning
For they see no future at all
As lost as people could be,
Aimless faces wander around,
Not one soul seems free,
Seemed like everyone just wanted to be found.

As the sun grew brighter,
More people rose.
From a war that lasted decades,
With hopes to pick up the pieces
And start life just where they,
Let it go.

About the Author

Anusha Sridharan is a software engineer by profession and a writer by heart. She loves making cards for people and art woos her like nothing else. She is also a passionate photographer and a regular blogger. She is very much interested to experiment with different genre of books and has contributed poems to StoryMirror's previous publication "Whistling Silence" and Lapsus Creations' Happy writers anthology - "Treasury". She keenly participates in poetry competitions and literature festivals.

A Simple What To That

By Anusha Sridharan

A simple what to that is a 'that' that starts with a 'what?'
A real speaking 'that' answers your 'what(s)!'
Consider this sentence, 'Everything that makes you, makes you
vulnerable to the one that you are!'
So, what exactly is that 'that'?

Sometimes that(s) are far more questioning than the what(s).
Many of the that(s) take you to the newer what(s).
The more you scout on a what, the more jarred you will be
with your that.
'What is that, that questions your what when
the what of yours ends with a that?'
Similarly, 'That is 'what' when the 'what' is a 'that' turned 'what'
when 'what' was 'that' masked with 'what'.'

My what(s) and that(s) are scattered.
Some what(s) and that(s) are distinct and others are
just too inter linked to clearly distinguish between
'which is what' and 'which is that'.
The voids between the what(s) and that(s)
are the answers attached to the reason of
your what(s) that are justified with your that(s).
In the end ask yourself, 'which is that 'that' that
answered your 'what'?

About the Author

Having a passion for writing from her very childhood, **Swaty** is a professional content writer from 8 years and provides SEO contents for various businesses. Her work has been published in websites like ezinearticles.com, sooperarticles.com, articlebase.com and so on. However, she has been writing poems and stories since the age of 6, her first work being published in the school's magazine during that time. She has been publishing her work on several online websites and local newspapers ever since. Her writings reflect much of her experiences and struggles with life every day, as she channelizes her thoughts through the words. She says writing is what gives her strength and keeps her alive and kicking. You can go through some of her writings in her personal blog at www.swatysinghworld.blogspot.com.

I Wish I Could Finish It All

By Swaty Singh

I wish I was never born,
I wish I was not known!
I am troublesome that's what they say,
I hope they will be happy if I go away…

I am imperfect I know,
I am immature however so,
Unaccepted to the many in the row,
I hope I could soon go!

This world's wrath I can take no more,
Every new day gets unbearably sore.
I wish I could end this all,
I wish I could cut all this small.

They say we cannot go before time
But what if tired of life I'm?
I wish I could just give up on life;
I wish I could go away from this strife!

I do not know how much I can bear,
It seems dark and impossible to stare.
I wish I could just cut it small!
I wish I could finish it once and for all !!!!!

About the Author

Aditya has been a technical writer by profession for more than 4 years now. It involves explaining highly technical concepts in a simple language understandable by the target audience in the IT industry. Currently based in Sydney, he also works freelance on proof-reading and editing assignments. When he is not busy writing, Aditya also enjoys shooting pictures and videos for his Instagram account. Check it out at https://www.instagram.com/adityaghaisas/.

Maybe Someday

By Aditya Ghaisas

Maybe
Someday, there won't be wars,
All this blood will not be lost.
We'll realize how much it all cost
Not only the pennies or the lives,
The loss of humanity that we'll all have caused.

Maybe
Someday, we'll stop murdering the future
The Aylans and the Omrans, our own
Too young to grasp the horrors we have grown
In this beautiful world of ours, our precious abode
Marred by violence, run by criminal crowns.

Maybe
Someday, there will be peace all around,
When weapons will only be in the chapters on history.
Lost in the annals of the terrible past, the mystery
Of why we chose to hate rather than love aloud
And why we let them burn it to the ground.

Maybe one day, there won't be wars,
All this blood will not be lost.

About the Author

Munni Banerjee is an Indian storyteller, poet, writer, illustrator, traveller and a spiritual healer who stays at Delhi with her husband, two sons, a cat and her kittens. She was born in Assam to a humble family. Her father was an Air Force veteran. She herself has experiences of working with corporates before being a mother. She loves travelling to the mighty Himalayas being a nature lover. She has been offering support and care to cancer patients and their caregivers with love and empathy. Munni Banerjee has been writing poems and blogs since quite sometime. She hopes to continue writing expressing herself with poetry, quotes and songs of different styles in future.

A Salute To Our Soldiers

By Munni Banerjee

Bold and brave your eyes
So full of love for the nation,
Courage in each and every breath
Blood you shed with pride.

No pain that can stop you
Obstacles bother you never,
Do or die the attitude
Your mind cannot be shaken ever.

Without fear or doubts in mind
Marching ahead to face,
Enemies who harm face the wrath of
True soldiers in an unstoppable pace.

I bow to thank your selfless service
For you I sleep each night safe,
Your courage shields us nationwide
Salute in love and gratitude.

About the Author

Leenu believes that 'It is too early to talk about myself'. 'Want to know me? Read me,' she says.

An Addict's Lament

By Leenu

My soulmate
companion
heart's desire
my pride
there was a time
you never left my
side

My window to the world
through your ears I heard
when I saw, it was
through your eyes
alas, my life ended
with your sudden
demise

Snatched away
by a gruesome fall
you were gone, and
no matter how I tried
never to return, although
I prayed, begged, pleaded
cried

Bereft of your touch
I am lost
contactless
filled with dread
curled up alone
in our once-shared
bed

Desolate, distraught
with no one beside
hurtling towards
No Friends zone
lost to the world
without you Sweet Beloved
*my*Phone

About the Author

Masoom is an IT professional during the day, while a writer at night. He enjoys blogging and shares his poetry, movie reviews and opinions on his blog sprinklinglife.com. Fiction always brings out a child's curiosity in him and he feels Poetry is the thoughts that we breathe. Having an inherent interest in poetry during his early school days, Masoom has developed an uncanny ability to transform abstract images into surprisingly charming piece of poetry. He someday aspires to publish his own anthology of sonnets.

In The Realm Of A Book

By Masoom Vyas

Under the light, beneath the reality, I live.
Layers of lifelessness surround me
Yet, I survive, I laugh, I cry, I feel free.
There are no clouds, neither does it rain
Yet I feel the chill, I get wet again, and again.
A single source of light tries its best to glow,
Yet I feel the sun shines bright, the wind flows.

Hours turn to days, and days turn to months
And I hear no sound from the distant reality,
Too distant you would think, too near I believe.
And I see no face, I see no smile...
Yet, I am in a carnival, spanning over a mile.
Filled with joyous humans, honest humans,
As alive as they have ever been, pure humans...

The drums roll, the trumpets hump, it's a celebration...
I hear the cheers, I hear the claps.
I am glad I reached here dodging all the traps.
Oh, a hero's welcome awaits me,
True to my-self I feel, as true as I've ever been...
I am in a world, that's written with emotion's ink.
And as much as I look at it, I try not to blink.

About the Author

Robin created his first poem "Olive Ridleys" for the school magazine "Buds & Blossoms" in the year 2006, and since then been a regular contributor for various magazines, newsletters and distinguished occasions as recitals. He is passionate and unique about capturing the different natural sensations that a soul expresses and experiences in the diverse walks of life. His educational experience in engineering and management has given him an extensive base to approach topics with insightful sensitivity and creative imagination. He has also authored a book called "Soulful Treasure" – An Anthology of Poems, which earned fame for its spontaneity in thoughts, heartfelt emotions, wide variety of themes and the ability to travel with the budding writer. You may explore more about his works at fb.me/robinjohnsoulfultreasure.

A Tender Bud

– Respect For Womankind

By Robin John

Pleasant days and cheerful nights just rolled ahead,
Sighting her angelic smiles from the cradle bed.
Thereafter, with each moment of care and utmost love;
They sweated and knelt down praying for blessings from above.

Never did they care for their very own world,
But, every heartbeat whispered for their beloved girl.
Peace and Joy overflowed in the beautiful house,
Until that one day when the lustful demon did arouse.

Dead at heart and a soul so wild,
He clutched by force the poor little child.
Perplexed! Right or wrong, she hardly knew the choice,
So she moaned, "It pains". Her only possible voice.

Helpless! She fell ruined and trampled on the ground,
He didn't want to spare the life though drenching in
her crying sound.
Can no supreme power stop this act so gruesome?
Wildly crushing a tender bud, before it can even blossom.

The lustful monster destroying fellow human of his own image,
Is only beast personified, but never called HUMAN at any stage.
Doubtlessly deserving to be punished and alleged to be dead,
Yet, can the dreams of the lovable family
be brought back instead.

The innocent soul blindly believes your sugar coated words,
Relating you like an elderly brother with kindness towards.
Easy deceit played on the faultless kid to earn such a shame!
That our whole splendid nation suffers a very awful name.

Forgiveness can be a chance for a burning crime,
But this devastating rape culture, becomes unpardonable
at any time.
We ought to rise, strengthening law and fighting for good.
As there's no shame proclaiming
"All Femininity is the symbol of Motherhood".

Friendship, Love, Lust or Care;
A righteous heart feels, and knows what to share.
Whatsoever, talents and traits can only win anyone
the greatest fan;
But "Respect for Womankind" shall alone make someone
A Complete Man.

About the Author

Akshat works as an auditor with a multi-national corporation. He is a chartered accountant by profession but literature comes naturally to him as son of two professors in literature. Apart from writing poetry and short stories both in Hindi and English language, he is also has interests in photography and active blogging. In his writings he presents the dilemmas of post-modern world and boldly shares his understanding of philosophy of life and strives to create sustainable social relationships and structures.

The New Year Resolution

By Akshat Shahi

As the year ends with the setting sun
I witness the fading red scene
And raise my arms to resolve
And be the same this year as well

I will not call for beautiful little birds
Who fly beyond the forbidden walls
Do not even know if they still flap
As recited in my grandma's tales

I will not long for the jungle's beasts
Mammoths, Dodos and Saber tooths
Who never saw a rising new Gregorian year
Not even the rhinos, tiger and gorillas
Who might not see the next rising year
I will let the smug souls live in peace
With their paradise on their screens

I will not force them out in the open
To witness the clouds of smoke and smell
I will not ask god to forgive my sins
Nor will I heal the broken hearts
I not cry like a kid on my silly mistakes
Nor will I resolve to change an inch

This year I will be a good soldier from the past
Fighting for pride, possession and polarized affinities
I will be a man of virtue as proclaimed last year
By the peers, seers and the market men
Who will be one by the rising sun

I will follow the man shouting on the screen
And build a new world of peaceful lull this year
With no wars in sandy land and no dictators in the east
No new kid to die on the beach and
No more boats with refugees to breach
There turn is over for the ultimate peace
This year they will find new lands for resurrection

I will join the forces for the sake of world peace
And continue to fight till the end of the world
With the peers, seers and the market men
All of them will fight with me and against me
The old settlers from the last war
And the new refugees from restructured lands
The blood will spill and virtues dies
Be it that way let us end it all this year
May be a new world and a god follows next year.

About the Author

Sharon is a student of history. Writing struck her when she won a creative writing contest in school by accident. She has worked for NGOs such as Teach for Green during her time as a bored student in Delhi University. She finds her ability to write amusing and spends a Saturday night musing over Fitzgerald and Orwell. She wishes to pursue a career in education.

Sightless By Choice

By Sharon

"2 Muslims killed in a Hindu rally,"
Blared the early morning news prior the Azaan,
Opening the eyes adjusted to a blue bodied god.
Mocking the monkey after their daily namaz,
But waking up to its remembrance,
As the mandir performed its quotidian rituals.

"Killings in the name of honor,"
Ran the evening news,
Because the biggest crime now was falling in love,
Without religious hindrance.

Fighting over right and wrong,
Over faith and loyalty,
Over the holy words of Koran,
And the copious versions of Hindu mythology,
With lacking shrewdness within themselves.

By what right do the Hindus claim this land,
By what right do they call this
their god, father and mother land.
Which part of the Koran calls the killing
in the name of religion a duty?
And which Mighty Hindu Book judges the loyalty of Muslims?

In this apocalyptic age,
The message of unity is long gone,
The message of destiny is lost,
Trust, love and faith misplaced in the void,
Leaving this sighted mankind sightless by choice.

About the Author

Sudhendu is a software engineer by profession for whom writing is a twin passion along with music and for whom both of these art-forms play a complementary role in his quest for self-expression. He is a student of Indian Classical Music and Indian Aesthetics and has a PG diploma in Indian Aesthetics from Jnanapravah in Mumbai. His fondness of aesthetics motivates him to maintain an artful approach both in his technical writings in the work space as well as when he is writing for his passion. His work reflects subtly as well as emphatically on the prevailing gender bias and the disparity in our society. Some of his work can be found online on StoryMirror and in the Facebook page 'Digbhrashtas'.

The Flute

By Sudhendu Chattopadhyaya

It was 6 am in the morning when the cawing woke me up.
By the time I sat with the *tanpura*,
The pigeons had made an audience.
My voice was croaky as usual,
And the audience had started their slow brooding.
With a final squawk I managed to croon a clear *Sa*
And received some encouraging flaps.

The teacher's words came back to me.
"You are a bit sharp", was her retort.
She asked the child to sing.
His voice, a soft husky conch,
made me think of a rill amid quietness somewhere.
I remembered the old family record
That had me chirping like a young nestling.
It had you too...
Like thin curls of smoke burning out of a joss stick.

Once when I had tried to woo a cuckoo;
imitating its plaintive search,
You had stopped me, saying that I was deluding the lovers.
So I had gone back to imitating yours'.
The class-teacher of my class had liked it back then.

He let me sing in the choir.
He said it blended well with the girls'.
And just to prove him wrong,
I tried singing louder than all.

When I reached the Nishad,
I seemed to miss the pitch yet again.
I looked imploringly into your dove shaped eyes.
You stood silently holding your flute,
Your eyes cast down.
You seemed like a memory of an inanimate past…
Then suddenly I heard the cuckoo back in the balcony.
I ran for him
And fluttered into the sky.

About the Author

Supreet is a Poet, Logophile and an Engineer. Her first stint in poetry was at the age of 12 and she continues to voice her envisaging skills in prose and rhymes. Her diligence in choice of words / expressions is a peculiarity seen in all her writings which are mostly titled in Greek / other dialects as her trademark style. Shetty's winning poetry, "Meraki" which also marks her debut as a published author has been immensely celebrated and applauded along with a viewership of more than 20K. Her recent writing includes "Saudade" which is a juxtapose in melancholy & happiness.

...Meraki - Love Begins...

By Supreet Shekhar Yashodha Shetty

Looking through the window, I realized life is mysterious,
After all, it fluctuated being ethical and boisterous;

My heart sets on fire when I'm not in your story,
But I believe, all this while our love will get victory;

These hiccups shall only venture to strengthen us,
As my loyalty and faith remains to be sonorous;

Nothing can drift us apart, as I thrive to be your shadow,
Walking at par with you through life's every meadow;

There are times when things we see may not be actual,
But whichever way you perceive, my love shall remain perpetual;

It hurts to know when you seek distance,
As my heart gets chocked in your absence;

Perhaps one seeks reply in isolation,
When our thoughts are not immune to any fluctuation;

As I lean on the lonely clouds of paradise,
I believe that these testing times shall only enrich and make us wise;

Looking through the window I realized life is mysterious,
After all it fluctuated being ethical and boisterous.

About the Author

Sukriti Chawla has been a member of the DPSI Social Services Club for over an year. Currently a student of Grade 10, she has written for the school magazine and has participated in numerous writing competitions. Learn more about the thoughts of this evolving writer and aspiring human rights activist by visiting her blog at speculationsofanimperfectmind.home.blog

What If I Didn't?

By Sukriti Chawla

They told me I had to be slim
And I obliged
They told me I had to cover skin
And I obliged

They wanted me to look beautiful
And I painted my skin in shades of lies
They wanted me to be good
And I painted my soul with layers of disguise

They wanted me to live
But all I could do was survive
And in collars of expectations strive
They wanted me to obey
So I never was astray
And followed their way

Until the rules threatened to choke me
And it was all I could do to not flee
Fallen prey to people's whims
I endured until my spirit dimmed

None stood for me
And before I could foresee
The next had already been guaranteed
To be the following breed
Of more women indeed
Expected to bleed
For yet more people's needs

About the Author

Yamika Gandhi is 18 years old and has finally escaped from DPS Dwarka, Delhi. She frequently writes on an orange colored website called Wattpad with the username @Cat_Walker and tries to sing on her instagram page that goes by her name. She hasn't won many contests before but well, somehow, here her poem is. Her only other achievement is that she was the class monitor in eighth grade.

Mirror

By Yamika Gandhi

The girl stared at me
From her position on
The bathroom floor.
I stared back.

She hugged her knees tightly
Her hair was stuck to her teary face
She looked at the knife
On the bathroom floor.
I looked at it too.

"Ugh!" she said suddenly,
And threw her hairbrush at me.
I cracked into a million pieces
And the shards fell
Onto the bathroom floor.
But I could still see her.

"I'm going to end my ugliness!" she said.
She picked up thc knife,
Pricked her finger.
A single drop of blood
Dripped onto the bathroom floor.
I could do nothing.

I was just a mirror after all,
Broken, like her.
I could not show her
How beautiful she was,
Because I could not reflect her soul.

The knife cut deep into her wrist,
Blood spurted onto the clothes she wore,
She fell down in a pool of red,
Onto the bathroom floor.

Here's a thought:
The things that you say
May leave scars that don't fade away
How about tasting your words
Before you spit them out?

About the Author

Deepa Lakshmi Ramesh started writing when she discovered the 'Best Listener' as a non-living thing. She loves to search for poetry in the mundane happenings. She helps writing for the lovesick people. She write to heal the lovelorn people. Her goal is to become the 'Best healer through words'. She would be contented for the purpose of her existence, if she changes the life of at least one human being through her writing. She has contributed as an author in an anthology named 'Memoirs of Teenage'. You can find more of her creation on yourquote.

11:30 PM

By Deepu Ramesh

I stand near a half broken window pane,
with the wall supporting my back.
As I was fully broken,
with no one to catch my back.

I could feel the salty breeze in my face,
the air left me with a salty touch.
As it brushed the memories of the list of people
who left me in the middle,
to make my life bi(e)tter.

The road was empty without any human intervention
like my mind,
as it travels down to the abyss of emptiness.

At the distant there was one who was fixing his scooter
to reach the destination,
at the same time I was bewildered equally,
with the broken pieces of my life.
As I was desperately solving to fix and move forward.

The pine tree stands tall, inspite of the blow of fierce winds.
I felt proud at myself that moment,
though life has knocked me every single time.
I was determined enough to get up.

An exhausted cow was walking slowly, at the side of the road
to reach a destination it never knew.
After a day's work, when my body begs to lie.
I still chose to think about the memories of the person
who changed tracks,
in search of a new destination.

I could hear crickets chirping the typical dusk music.
Deep and deep inside,
my heart whispers the tone of melancholy.

At the place I stand, I could see two roads
that led to two different places.
I was there standing with my pen and diary, scribbling this.
Besides a frustrated Monday blues,
to complete the tasks assigned.

About the Author

Sita has studied Psychotherapy and practiced in Mumbai for three years before migrating to Australia in 2008. She has been a member of a Writers' Group in Melbourne for two years and has completed three Online Writers' Courses provided by University of Iowa. With five decades of life behind her, she is currently writing a book about Mumbai and its people, a subject she knows best having lived there most of her life.

Un-belong

By Sita Sai

Through the window pierced
Her pointless stare

Among strange people
Her eyes gleamed of despair

She reminisced her heartbeat merge with thine
The delicacies you demanded
That she must dine

The love you sought
With kicks you fought

Ceaseless prompts of an offspring
Gelusil, her fancied drink

Throw ups and lie downs, her bustle
Then you appeared out of the canal
She breathed in your scent.

Your tiny hands clasped her little finger
Your benign eyes trusting

You both grew and grew
She grew more
And waited at the door

That which was not home but still called it
Your stingy life was squandered, not spent

She sought your little finger to hold
You pulled your hand back

She pushed herself into wet moss
You will get a call soon.

Sooner than soon
To say you were a burden to your cross.

About the Author

Harsh is currently working as an Assistant Vice President in one of the major international banks. He is the author of the book "How not to get hacked" and writes technical articles for VPNMentor. Although Harsh spends the majority of his time in the software and technology world, he loves to write poetry in his free time. He has many other diversified interests like playing cricket, palm reading, performing magic tricks, traveling and philosophy. Harsh can be found at his website www.harshmaurya.in

Who Am I

By Harsh Maurya

Who am I?
I am the seed of a blossom
Almost ready to cleanse the earth
With my fragrance without dearth
But someone thought me as a problem
So they crushed me and left me rotten

Who am I?
I am a tiny little needle
They compare me with a dagger
Say that it is better and sharper
I am delicate, dagger can't do what I can
It can't create, only gives wounds and pain

Who am I?
I am the leaf of a tree
Happy with all my family nearby
Until a wind takes me away in the sky
It forces me to follow it like a ghost
And then dumps me when I need it most

Who am I?
I am the planet Earth
I give life and nurture my children
Suffer pain and expect nothing in return

But my children humans have lost their way
Destroying me in the name of play
When I am dead, they will realize it too
Second mother won't love them like I do

Who am I under all this cover?
I am a girl, sister, wife and mother!!

About the Author

A Human resource person by profession, a poet and blogger by passion, **Swati Patil** works for a leading corporate company by day and spends her free time writing poems and blogs, predominantly on women diversity and love for children. Having done master's in business management as a career aspiration, Swati decided to divulge her decades old passion for literature after 13 years of being a people person and completed her Masters in English literature. The impulse to study has not stopped there, yet, and currently she is a research scholar specialising on interpretation of trauma in literature by select works of English and Non-English authors.

The Star

By Swati Patil

As I walk down the lane on a star studded night,
The moon casts a silvery shadow across the moor,
I stealthily approach my spot at the old oak,
Gazing at the skies, trying to find, and there is she,
Shining brightest, against the night sky.

A little angel, sanctified by beauty and grace,
She waves at me with a smile on her serene face,
Her halo demeaning the glow from moonlight,
With wings so grand that cherubs awe with plight.
Shining brightest, against the night sky.

Little blue eyes gleaming down at me,
"I am here mama", says Carol, my little girl,
Playing peek a do with the angles around,
I see my baby, dancing and singing,
Shining brightest, against the night sky.

Emotions sweep over me like the purple of night,
I see her happy and gay, enveloped in God's love,
Fred from the pain and suffering, far far away,
Making her mark amongst the constellations,
Shining brightest, against the night sky.

As the first light starts streams through the beautiful night,
She peeps through the clouds with a mischief smile,
Promising to return the next night. I get up to move,
Letting a tear fall through. Knowing I will see her soon,
Shining brightest, against the night sky. Every night!

About the Author

Prajakta Chaudhari wears many feathers in her cap. She is an engineer by education, software programmer by profession and writer by passion. A bibliophile with a quest for writing and obscure inclinations has stumbled onto the blog world to pen down her strong feminist voice. She is a wordsmith and known for her poetry. She explores her interest in writing on various topics like social women-centric issues, education, relationships through her blog and specializes in writing poems across difference genres. Apart from her personal blog, she has also contributed articles on different websites like timesofindia, womensweb, momespresso and StoryMirror. Visit her blog at https://prajaktachaudhari.wordpress.com/

To Working Mom, I Understand

By Prajakta Chaudhari

As a son, I appreciate all your sacrifice,
That goes into balancing personal and professional life.

I know what you go through every day,
Whether it is a weekend or weekday.
Dividing your time and energy,
Between work and family.

I try my best to help you with the chores one by one,
Sadly I realized, a mother's work is never done.
In between compromises and sacrifices,
Please find what is crucial to your happiness.

There is no right way or wrong way,
It is what is right for you in your situation that day.
I suggest replacing 'Should' with 'Could',
Trust me mom, it's all nice but not very good.

The 'Mom Guilt' is what you are suffering,
Especially when you can't afford something.
Understand that perfection and parenting is incongruous,
You get me and now I get you, me and us.

Please feel good and take pride,
I understand that being working mother is not an easy ride.

About the Author

Sheerali wears multiple hats at same time. She has more than 12 years of experience in Corporate and Education fields. She was working as a Banker for a decade in India and her quest for knowledge led her to pursue PhD in Management. She has always been a passionate writer since her school days and her articles and poetry have been published in prominent Newspapers and Magazines like Times of India, The Hindu and Aalav. Her Research Papers have also been published in reputed International Academic Journals. It is her strong belief that writing provides a much needed satisfaction for soul and mind. She further believes that it is essential to pass on knowledge to other people. She is a keen Social Activist and member of welfare Organizations like UNICEF and Breast Cancer Foundation NZ. Currently, Sheerali is working as a Management Lecturer in New Zealand and continues to pursue her dream of writing more and more.

Guardian Angel Forever

By Sheerali Arya

Rock solid was his hold,
Taught me to be confident and bold.

Worked tirelessly day and night,
Propelled me to stand up against any fight.

Was a proud man of few words,
Guided me to be unique and not one of herd.

Tough on outside but mellow within,
Learnt from him that humbleness is where it all begins.

One in a zillion persona he had,
Showed me compassion and to be never mad.

Pushed me to test all my limits with zeal,
Your absence has left a void never to heal.

Your memories leave me teary eyed,
After you, something inside me died.

Would travel to beyond to see you again,
Forgive me for the times when I was a pain.

Renowned is he still as man with a golden heart,
Balanced everything perfectly in his life's cart.

His love for all was an epitome of supreme sacrifice,
May you rest in peace forever in God's own dais.

About the Author

Ramachandra is an active writer on various online platforms and has a myriad collection of quotes and poems. He goes by the pen name Chaiwithpai which is also his Instagram handle. He has published quite a few articles on Hubpages and blogger. But when he realized short pieces are his forte, he switched to writing quotes. You can find his technical articles as well on Medium. In technical, he mostly writes on AEM and Angular. In general, he prefers to use analogy to raise awareness about social issues and human behavior. His most interesting poems are the क्या बताऊँ series in Hindi which is a humorous take on love and life.

An Ode To Mom And Dad

By Ramachandra Pai

You gave me birth, taught me to talk;
Holding my finger, you made me walk.
And then came friends, people of my age;
Slowly I moved to, my life's next stage.

Playing in the rain, I used to get ill;
But without any complaints, you nurtured me still.
Some things not to be done, was told by you;
Out of curiosity, I still used to do,

And then I came to you, bruised and battered;
You were there with me, always when it mattered.
Sacrifices you made, for my better future;
Gratitude to you, was still not in my nature,

Young and naive I was, nothing I knew;
You guided me throughout, till mature I grew.
Independent I became, took my own decision;
Your support was although there, there was never any cessation.

When upset I grew, it hurt you the most;
When happy I was, your joy knew no bounds.
A smile on my face, would make your day;
You never let any trouble, come my way.

Words are insufficient, to completely describe you;
For people like you, are extremely few.
Nothing much I can do, to repay your debt;
All I can do, is say 'Thank You',

Thank you mom, Thank you dad;
You are the best, anybody could ever have had.
Anybody could ever have had!

About the Author

Divya Raghunathan is a Content Writer in Mystery Monks, a reputed video-production company at Sarita Vihar. She is a Biotechnology post-graduate from VIT University. A self-confessed lover of English literature, music & fine arts, her poetic flair and quest for the higher-intellect encourage her to pursue multitudes. She was awarded 'Sahitya Pratibha' at the Kannur University Youth Fiesta 2011. Poetry for her is the ethereal beauty woven with powerful feelings stemming from the verisimilitude, the truth we seek & beyond them too. That divine aura which transforms darkness to light and love! Explore her little universe at: https://poetsutopia.wordpress.com/ and https://oculusignis.quora.com/.

Ruins

By Divya Raghunathan

Walking back from the temple…
Carrying a heart…
Filled with hopes and promises…
With the soothing morning breeze…
A companion… to me and Dad…
Matching his footsteps with us…
As we trod down, that familiar steep road…
While my hands, clasped tight to my father's secure fingers…
I could see his eyes…
Blessed with content…
Which radiated through me too…
Spreading a happiness that we both shared…
'Coz we knew …
We were here… at home…
Far from the chaos of our metropolitan life…
Yes! We were here… Where our heart,
Had built, its abode…

As we turned left…
In to a narrow-walled lane…
Of moss-covered laterite blocks…
I could see all those glimpses of childhood…
Rushing forth, to welcome me…

The aroma of the damp soil…
The swaying fronds of the coconut palms…
The stinging, yet, cherished pain…
Those pointed stones left on my bare foot…
The innocent charm of the wild flowers…
The lingering ripe smell of a pineapple crouched somewhere…
And whooshing sounds of the plantain chips…
Fried fresh, filling my ears on the other…

And now I could see it…
My longing eyes darting further…
Than my heavy-paced steps …
The battered roof that gave –
A statement of age…
Caved inwards from one side…
The cracks that bore themselves deeper…
In to the walls …
Pronounced… Just like the nostalgia within us…
The house… Our house…
That lay buried in the many layers of dust…
And the nuances of revived memories…
A territory, which was now,
Out – of – bounds… for us…
And desolation – its rightful owner…
No longer were the magnanimous 'Deodars…
Standing tall… To welcome me…

Instead I found myself, grieving…
At the chopped limbs of my faithful comrades…
The garden that thrived cheerfully…
In the caring hands of my Grandpa…
Was now a graveyard…
For the dry twigs, weeds and mangled stalks…
My favorite swing –
The sturdy bark of a coconut frond…

Was stashed away ropes-bereft…
Among the wild thickets in the corner, to the right.
My prompt feet carried me to the background…
In the hope that it, at least,
Wouldn't have changed …

The vast space of that ravished land…
Was being hammered on me…
As if each painful striking blow …
Was a reminder…
Of every single palm n plantain…
And the trees of mango, cashew and pepper…
On whose laps we were cradled…

The chikoos that grew right in front…
That all of us cousins would relish with glee…
The tender branches of the cashew tree…
Where we'd chatter away and swing…
The well, its waters…
Cold and sprinkling…
That blessed our morning showers…
Was now a doused sepulchre…
For the fallen leaves and insects…

I felt my hand tighten…
From my Dads' perturbed grasp…
May be he was reliving his childhood too…
And I knew I was right, when I saw…
Him breathing, frantic…
I also knew that he was,
Holding on to each and every end …
Of the broken strings…
Shattered memories of the days gone by…
Clutching all those broken pieces…
Close to his heart…

Helplessness that seemed to wade through,
Pointlessly…
Along with the ebbing pain…
That is when I turned to him and said –
"Perhaps the greatest misery Dad…
Is becoming a stranger,
In the land of our own…"

About the Author

Mahisha is a high-school student who writes mostly for herself. She has written articles and poems for school magazines and newspapers, but specially finds poetry as an escape from her daily routine. You may find more about her work in her monthly articles in the 'MyPaper' children's magazine where her writing reached a greater audience for the first time.

Farewell

By Mahisha Markandan

It was nearly a day since he had died.

A muted, hoarse wail leaked through the gaps
of the thickly crowded windows and door.
They parted as I approached.
There were no men inside; only my father,
muttering to the big box, sinking to his knees
as his shaking legs could no longer hold him.

Rough hands clutched mine, and laser eyes followed me
as I weaved my way through, when
my grandmother pulled me into her lap,
to whisper nonsense.

From there I saw, for the first time, beneath the fresh flowers,
the frail, limp body of my grandfather.

He looked quite peaceful for a dead man:
tender lids shut forever to this beautiful reality,
hearing no more the moaning cries of the living.
His thick, grey moustache was still visible,
a fearsome cover, as he smiled in his slumber,
though it always made me laugh. Even then.
I was not sad to see him nap; only my hands
itched to throw his blanket over the coffin's cold.

Yet, a single tear spilled from my eye,
rolled down my cheek, and
dried before it hit the floor.
I still wonder, why?

A while later, a soft silence settled over the parade;
only the gravel crunching under the village's soles echoed the truth.
A greater man never walked the streets, they said.
Still, the march led on to the graveyard.

They stopped us before we could enter, afraid of the
women's whimpers and howls.
We were to moan elsewhere,
so half his admirers abandoned him.

Rounding the bend, I saw ash,
sifting along the August breeze, fairly serene;
and asked the bones, lovingly hidden:
who would call back the mirth, now goodbye bidden?

About the Author

Mandeep Singh writes various genres of poetry (dominantly gay romance) and is into content writing as well. Presently working with StoryMirror, Dark University, Pixels Club and TEDx DAV Chandigarh, being his last year of graduation in arts-cum-education. He has got his poems published at leavesofink, DelhiPoetrySlam. His works (poems) include Habits, What's the worst, Guilty Pleasure, A Cherished Desire and many more. He aspires to be an anonymous inspiration for the youth struggling with sexuality.

A Girl's Cry For Help!!!!!!!

By Mandeep Singh

You kill me even before I'm born
I can't speak or move cuz inside I'm torn
You don't let me shout a cry
Outside you're ready with a sword trying to pry

For your sons, you act so indiscriminate
You ain't the Lord, you've no right to decide my fate
Sometimes I wonder, is it really you?
You're my devil or angel, I guess both suit you

I won't ask for, neither your property nor thy wealth
I'll sit in the corner, eat only enough for health
I won't bring disgrace, to your self-respect
I'll follow your orders, as if I'm being punished for a theft

Why I have to go through, all this?
Why your eyes don't get wet, when you do it?

What I'm supposed to feel like?
Whether I'm a human or living an animal's life?

I dream of, you embracing me when I'm a kid
Playing the game, of finding the things you intentionally hid

About the Author

Priya Singh is a student of class 12 at D. A. V Public School. She is into writing from 4 years. Other than poetry, she also writes stories and novels. She is active on wattapad as a sci-fi writer and right now she is working on one of her novel. Also she writes one-liners and quotes on yourquote. She is a member of Writers helping writers and Indie author group on facebook. Generally she writes her poems in freestyle. She has taken Science as her major subject in school.

Finding Heaven

By Priya Singh

Finding Clues,
I went through those dusky lanes,
Which were covered with morning mist.
I tiptoed, not to make any noise.
And went with a throbbing heart to find,
To find her;

This lane made many memories to flood out in my eyes.
My childhood, my friends.......
and my house, which has now turned into a dismal state.
With broken windows and wild flowers covering it wholly,
Almost making a scene of haunted house.
I, with terrible feeling got inside through the broken fence wall,
And tapped at the door.

From inside came a very old woman with her skin hanging,
And a small stick to support her.
She, when saw me, hugged me with all her might.
My hands automatically moved towards her bended curves.
As I hugged her, I felt my tears automatically falling down
streaming through my eyes and then landing on her back.
She freed me after about an hour.

Her tears,
Perhaps the tears of happiness flowed down her cheeks.
She was about to say something,
But unknowingly my crooked voice cutting her words uttered "MA".
She paused for a while,
And her eyes again, were filled with fresh tears.
She laid me through the roughly cleaned balcony to a room
which was tried very hard to keep clean.

As she sat on the bed I laid my head in her lap,
Which was filled with the warmth of motherly love;
Which was much more comforting than the heaven's cool breeze.

Her magical hands barely let my eyes to be open for
more than a second.
I hugged her tightly, before going for a sleep and
promised her that I will never betray her now.
At that promise, she just refilled her eyes with fresh tears.

About the Author

Rajen Mehta is a retired convent high school teacher. Though he is B.A. and B.Ed., he still thinks himself as a KG student in field of poetry. And it is true because his very few works have been published in various anthologies and platforms. His humorous blogs have been published in websites like WWH (active in 2008), word shots in Writer's Bag, etc. Recently he is active on Facebook with 'LOL of the Day' as daily one liners.

Busy Children

By Rajen Mehta

It's play time,
And children are not
At Children's corner!
Where are they?
Some of them may be
Busy in drudgery work,
To earn their bread!
Some may busy in playing
Outdoor games on videos!
Some may be playing Outdoor games in shooting
For TV serials!

Or some may be discussing on global warming,
Or on 'playing outdoor games
Is outdated culture',
In TV talk shows!
Or some may be taking
Shooting training
To save so called religion!
Or some may be busy
In shaving heads,
To turn into monks!

But I am damn sure that,
Rest of them are busy
In completing their
School homework
Given by 7 subject's teachers!

About the Author

Shamsher Singh is a technocrat turned teacher whose passion for teaching drives him. Having experience in core domains as well as in software, he has now switched over to teaching and is vigorously active in mentoring and nurturing students for IIT - JEE as well as guiding them about different career prospects. Also, his interests ranges from writing poetry, reviewing, interviewing, story writing etc. Presently he is associated with The Mahabodhi Tree (Bodhgaya) as a Maths Faculty. Many of my writings have found place in esteemed national as well as international journals both online as well as in print.

Mother - The God On Earth

By Shamsher Singh

Sheltered in the womb
The world was all unknown
I was living in your realm
With the plethora of joy, hope, love and dreams

I was pondering in ignorance
For I was the wizard of absolute
I was all crumbling with biases
Yet I was in a slumber for I was in God's arena

Ready to rejoice with unfolded mysteries
For With your breaths
I was alive
For With your thoughts

I was thoughtless with blueprints of thoughts mapped
I was all there as a part of you
To erupt with a zeal
With the thirst to see my bifurcated soul

I opened my eyes with a cry
Yet with a smile in heart
For the pain of bifurcation was unbearable
Yet there was the schism with unsaid promise

The divine flow swapped to find the merge
With an unknown console, that whispered
You are blessed to be in the lap of the mother
And further slower was the whisper in my ears that echoed
"Mother – the god on earth!
You are blessed!"

About the Author

"Life heed you to the way it turns on"

A Software Engineer started her journey from city of dreams "Mumbai" to forge her identity. Somewhere amidst the zippy pace of the city she discovered a blossoming wordsmith within her. Just as her name "**Manmee**t" i.e "Friend of mind", this emotive poem clearly acquaints you with the feeling that highlights the recondite support of a "Father".

Dad

By Manmeet Arora

When I step down into the world, you were there to praise ..
When I was ready to take a step, you were there to hold ...

When I grown up, you were there to teach...
When I was ready to leave, you were there to encourage...

When I was alone, you were there to accompany ..
When I felt disheartened, you were there to console...

No matter what life has chosen..
No matter how tough it seems..
But You're and always special beyond compare...

Dedicated to The Man, who we called it as "DAD"...